THE
ROMANCE
OF
Ruth

THE
ROMANCE
OF
Ruth

GEORGE E. GARDINER

KREGEL PUBLICATIONS
Grand Rapids, MI 49501

The Romance of Ruth by George E. Gardiner. Copyright ©
1977 by Kregel Publications, a division of Kregel, Inc. All
rights reserved.

Library of Congress Cataloging in Publication Data

Gardiner, George E.
    The Romance of Ruth.

    1. Ruth (Biblical character). 2. Bible. O.T. —
Bibliography. I. Title.
BS580.R8G37 222'.35'0924 [B]   77-79187
ISBN 0-8254-2718-5
Printed in the United States of America

CONTENTS

PREFACE

In response to many requests from his church members, a busy pastor has written this book. The material was originally presented as a series of Sunday morning messages and was intended for the person in the pew, rather than the theologian. The response to the messages was gratifying.

So, the perils of extemporaneous speech having been removed, and the contents reduced to only that which is important, this resultant book is shared with the reading public.

In preparation for the preaching series, I was interested to discover how few books have been written about Ruth. In spite of the fact that her story is one of the best-known Bible stories, and although her experience provides a striking illustration of the Biblical doctrine of salvation; the book of Ruth has suffered from neglect by writers. This small volume, in no way, is an attempt to fill the void. But if it creates an interest in one heart, and out of that interest someone begins to explore this beautiful Old Testament book of Ruth; all the effort will have been worthwhile.

George E. Gardiner

IT WAS THE WORST
OF TIMES

Ruth 1: 1-5

1 Now it came to pass in the days when the judges ruled, that there was a famine in the land. And a certain
man of Beth-lehem-judah went to sojourn in the
country of Moab, he, and his wife, and his two sons.

2 And the name of the man was E-lim-e-lech, and the
name of his wife Na-o-mi, and the name of his two
sons Mah-lon and Chi-li-on, Eph-ra-thites of Beth-
lehem-judah. And they came into the country of
Moab, and continued there.

3 And E-lim-e-lech Na-o-mi's husband died; and she
was left, and her two sons.

4 And they took them wives of the women of Moab;
the name of the one was Or-pah, and the name of the
other Ruth: and they dwelled there about ten years.

5 And Mah-lon and Chi-li-on died also both of them;
and the woman was left of her two sons and her husband.

1

IT WAS THE WORST OF TIMES

It was the worst of times in Israel — how bad it was can be seen by referring back to the last statement in the Book of Judges, "every man did that which was right in his own eyes." What that means can be understood by reading the whole Book of Judges. The story is one of apostasy, anarchy, brutality and bloodshed as it always is when unregenerate man is unrestrained and each is doing "his own thing."

The situation with Israel had not always been so. There were the slavery days in Egypt — five centuries of grinding despotism. Then when God delivered Israel from Egypt, Moses was "king" (Deuteronomy 33:5). When Moses died, Joshua took over the rulership and rebels were put to death. The judges took over when Joshua died, and a truly permissive society began to emerge, "every man did that which was right in his own eyes."

What an opportunity to show how mankind progresses when completely free — free of God and man, but it didn't work out that way; the greater Israel's freedom, the deeper their bondage became. The more they did as they pleased, the less pleased they were with what they did. The more they became what they wanted to be, the less they wanted to be what they became. What should have been a millenium, became pandemonium.

How could it happen? Why did it happen? The answer is seen in one phrase, repeated four times in Judges, "there was no king." In chapter seventeen, verse six, we read, "no king," followed by the story of a Levite prostituting his office for money and security. In chapter eighteen, verse one, we note, "no king," followed by strife among the tribes. In chapter nineteen, verse one, again we read, "no king," followed by an incident of shocking brutality and immorality. In chapter twenty-one, verse twenty-five, we note, "no king," which sums up the whole, ugly picture. Who was the missing king? God! His benevolent yoke had been thrown off in the name of freedom, liberty, and accommodation to humanity. The inevitable chaos resulted! It was indeed the worst of times.

In such a time, we come to Ruth, the eighth book of the Bible. Eight is the number of new beginnings in the Scriptures. This brief, but beautiful, story shows us that even in the darkest of times, God is not idle, all is not lost, and the Almighty always has a remnant reserved unto Himself. Ruth is the sunrise after a dark night of sin, immorality, and corruption. Ruth lifts the curtain just enough for us to see the unshaken God, directing the drama of the ages on the stage of earth with actors who are not fully aware of where their parts fit into the script.

The Unshaken God

When everyone seemed to have deserted the faith of the fathers, God had His remnant — a fact seen all through both the Bible and secular history.

In the days before the flood, there were Enoch and Noah.

In the days of the Tower of Babel, there was Abram in Ur of Chaldee.

When Israel was being scourged with captivity and foreign occupation, there was Jeremiah.

Behind the "curtains" of our day, iron and bamboo, there are those "who have not bowed the knee to Baal."

So in the Book of Ruth, there are Boaz and his reapers who greet each other with, "the Lord bless you" (Ruth 2:4).

It was the worst of times; but God was still Sovereign, sin was still restrained, and Satan was still limited in what he could do.

God has His remnant in Israel.

He also had a *plan* for victory. The Book of Judges closes with the dirge, "There was no king," but Ruth closes with a promise, "Jesse begat David" — the link in the lineage through which Messiah would come! And God was working His plan so inconspicuously — a widow, from a cursed race, who happened to wander into Boaz's field. Where is the high drama or good public relations in that? The nation wasn't even aware that anything unusual was going on! But God was watching and working out His purpose in the worst of times.

How strangely He did so.

The Strange Ways Of God

God's plan began with a failure, Elimelech, whose name means, "'My God is king," who by his actions denied his name when famine came. He, with his wife Naomi, bundled up his two sons and left Bethlehem "the house of bread" for Moab, a land of people under a curse — there to die and be buried alongside both his children. What an unlikely soil in which to plant the seed of a miracle! Yet this is where God began.

His plan continued with a pagan — Ruth, a Moabitess who married one of Elimelech's sons, then buried him beside his father. A member of a race which began in incest (Genesis 19), disrupted the journey of Israel from Egypt to Canaan, and was under the curse of God (Deuteronomy 23:3-6). God took this woman from the lowest of conditions and raised her to the highest of privileges — an ancestress of the Messiah!

And He is still doing it!

We were failures like Elimelech. We couldn't please God or keep His law. We had no righteousness He could accept, indeed our righteousness was as "filthy rags" (Isaiah 64:6).

We were pagans, "born in sin and shapen in iniquity," "children of wrath" (Ephesians 2:3). Instead of loin cloths, we wear suits and dresses. Instead of crude idols of wood and stone, we worshiped idols of chrome and plastic, but we were pagans. The word comes from the Latin word "paganus, outsider" and that is what we were.

> "That at that time ye were without Christ, being aliens from the commonwealth of Israel, and strangers from the covenants of promise, having no hope, and without God in the world" (Ephesians 2:12).

"But God . . ." (Ephesians 2:4).

What a blessed phrase, introducing the truth that though we were failures, pagans, helpless, and defiled, God raised us and saved us, "For by grace ye are saved through faith and that not of yourselves, it is the gift of God" (Ephesians 2:8).

The story of Ruth is the story of a God, Who is not frustrated by the failure of an instrument or the poor quality of the material with which He has to work. He continues to work out details of His plan, even in the worst of times.

THE REMARKABLE RUMOR

6 Then she arose with her daughters in law, that she might return from from the country of Moab: for she had heard in the country of Moab how that the LORD had visited his people in giving them bread.

7 Wherefore she went forth out of the place where she was, and her two daughters in law with her; and they went on the way to return unto the land of Judah.

8 And Na-o-mi said unto her two daughters in law, Go, return each to her mother's house: the LORD deal kindly with you, as ye have dealt with the dead, and with me.

9 The LORD grant you that ye may find rest, each of you in the house of her husband. Then she kissed them; and they lifted up their voice, and wept.

10 And they said unto her, Surely we will return with thee unto thy people.

11 And Na-o-mi said, Turn again, my daughters: why will ye go with me? are there yet any more sons in my womb, that they may be your husbands?

12 Turn again, my daughters, go your way; for I am too old to have an husband. If I should say, I have hope, if I should have an husband also tonight, and should also bear sons;

13 Would ye tarry for them till they were grown? would ye stay for them from having husbands? nay, my daughters; for it grieveth me much for your sakes that the hand of the LORD is gone out against me.

14 And they lifted up their voice, and wept again: and Or-pah kissed her mother in law; but Ruth clave unto her.

15 And she said, Behold, thy sister in law is gone back unto her people, and unto her gods: return thou after thy sister in law.

2

THE REMARKABLE RUMOR

Naomi was a bitter woman. "Don't call me Naomi 'pleasant,' call me Mara 'bitter,'" she said to her friends upon her return to Bethlehem. And why not? To avoid the famine which had gripped Israel, her husband, Elimelech, had taken her and their two sons from Bethlehem "the house of bread" to Moab, a land of people who were under the curse of God. In Moab, they found food, but at a price they had not expected to pay! Their sons married local girls — members of a cursed race. Elimelech took sick and died, soon both sons died, and Naomi found herself a childless widow — living among strangers, destitute, lonely, and bitter — "call me Mara."

Then the first ray of light and hope appeared. A remarkable rumor reached this lonely, bitter woman, "The Lord had visited His people in giving them bread." The famine was over back home in Bethlehem! She longed to go home. Do you think I could go back now? Wonder if anyone would remember me? How would I be received? God had shown His might in spite of the mistakes of men.

The Mistakes Of Man And The Might Of God

Elimelech had made mistakes; let us consider two of them.

First, he had turned his back on his inheritance because of a temporary situation. His name means, "My God is king." When his parents gave him the name, they recognized that Jehovah was the Sovereign of Israel and therefore responsible for the supply and protection of the nation. Joshua had reminded the people in his farewell address that "not one promise failed." But Elimelech forgot the truth of his name; and, by turning his back on Bethlehem "the house of bread," he testified, with his feet, that his God was not able to feed him and his family. If only he had remembered others, who had made similar mistakes — Lot sitting in the gate of Sodom, Abram running to Egypt during another famine — perhaps he would have realized that his path would lead to tragedy and heartbreak.

Second, he fled from the chastisement of God. It is no mere coincidence that verse one reads, " . . . In the days when the judges ruled, there was a famine . . . " Those days are described in the last verse of the Book of Judges, a picture of apostasy and anarchy! And, as happened before and afterward, the chastening rod fell upon the back of a disobedient and rebellious people.

Now, let's be clear in our thinking about the chastisement of God. God does not lose His temper and lash out at His children as some human parents do. His chastisement is not revenge or "tit-for-tat." Nor is it petty punishment. The chastisement of God is always in love: "whom the Lord *loveth* he chasteneth . . ." (Hebrews 12:6), and it is always to bring us to repentance and restoration. Israel had become disobedient and rebellious; and, when they would not respond to grace, the corrective rod of famine fell.

Elimelech would have been better off with the people of God in Bethlehem under judgment, than he was with the devil's crowd in Moab having his hunger satisfied. When God disciplines His own, they cannot escape by running to Moab. Elimelech died, his sons died, his family line was blotted out — a calamity to a Jew — and his wife was left a lonely, bitter stranger among the enemies of her people. As a wise man once said, "The mills of the gods grind slowly, but they grind exceedingly small."

How dark and dismal and depressing this story would be if it were to end with the mistakes of Elimelech. Thank God it doesn't! God, in marvelous might, was working, and the rumor reached Naomi, "The Lord had visited His people . . .." As Paul wrote to the Romans, "God Who quickeneth the dead, and calleth those things which be not as though they were" (Romans 4:17). Elimelech's household was one of the "things which be not", it was "dead"; but God had a plan which would make it forever remembered. The mistakes of Elimelech would be woven into the pattern of redemption for man, by the loom of God. God rules and overrules in the affairs of men and nations. Just what could He do to salvage His nation? What was His plan?

Rumor and Repentance

What was the rumor? The Lord had visited His people in giving them bread." How simple, yet how sublime. Here is good news in a plain wrapper. Men have a tendency to make the Gospel hard and complicated, at times incomprehensible; but Jesus said, "I am the bread of life," "If any man thirst, let him come unto me and drink," "Come unto me all ye who labor and are heavy laden and I will give you rest." Simple words, common experiences, everyday needs, food, drink, rest. No wonder little children so readily receive the Saviour. Naomi heard a simple rumor so succinctly, that she began packing for the journey, "The Lord had visited His people in giving them bread."

"Bread," sustenance, satisfaction. Bread speaks of home. Bethlehem was "the house of bread".

"Giving them bread" reminds us of a fact forgotten in this sophisticated day. It used to be that God sent the rain, now it happens by blind laws of meteorology. It used to be that God gave the harvest, now the fertilizer gets the credit. We are the poorer for having lost the truth contained in

Maltlie Babcock's poem,

"Back of the loaf is the snowy flour,
And back of the flour the mill,
And back of the mill is the wheat, and
   the shower,
And the sun, and the Father's will."

The Lord had visited His people, and there was bread in Bethlehem once again.

This rumor produced action by Naomi: "She arose . . . went on the way to return unto the land of Judah" (vss. 6,7).

Here is an accurate illustration of repentance. Naomi reversed the direction she and her husband had taken. She turned her back on Moab, the mistakes of the past, the graves of disobedience, as she turned toward the land which they should never have left.

We have a problem with repentance, because we often confuse it with penance. Penance comes from the Latin word for penalty. Penance is paying: Tears, self-denial, public humiliation all may be part of the price we pay. But repentance is basically a turning around, an "about face," a reversal of direction. Paul says that "godly sorrow *worketh* repentance," but sorrow is not in itself repentance. Naomi turned *from Moab to* Bethlehem, *from* disobedience *to* restoration, *from* sin *to* salvation. God always takes us *out* to bring us *in*. The "from" and "into" go together. That is repentance, and it produces wonder and witness.

The Wonder And The Witness

Think of the wonder of the news that reached Naomi in Moab. Hope had died and been buried in the three graves she visited. Her joy had soured into bitterness. Life was cruel, until the news came from Bethlehem; God had not forgotten His people, in Bethlehem there was bread to eat and homes to eat it in and families with which to enjoy it. All that she lacked in Moab was provided in Israel. Good news, gracious news, great news for a lonely, frustrated, bitter child of God, out of God's will, out of God's place, and away from God's people. It said to her "I can go back," "things can be different," "the Lord has visited His people."

So wonderful was the news that it produced a witness. Naomi's enthusiastic response carried her two daughters-in-law along with her. These young ladies had no memories of Bethlehem. The news of bread being provided there meant nothing to them, they were Moabites, enemies of Israel, strangers to Jehovah, yet they went along with Naomi. Why? It was the contagion of their mother-in-law's enthusiastic joy that caught their interest and moved their wills.

The best Christian witnesses are not the skilled debaters, the profound theologians, or those who retire from the world. The witness who impresses men is the one who is radiant with the wonder of God in Christ. Simon Peter was busy with his fish business; until his brother Andrew came running down the beach, breathlessly exclaiming, "We have found the Christ!'' The sound of Andrew's voice and the look on his face sent Peter's nets falling to the sand and his feet pounding after Andrew to see the One who generated such excitement in his brother's life. Something like that took place in Moab. What they heard from and saw in Naomi was so attractive that Ruth and Orpah were willing to pull up stakes, leave home, and journey to another country. The wonder had produced a witness. And the witness was effective.

So three widows went to the cemetery and stood weeping at three graves, then they began the long walk to Bethlehem. Somewhere, they had not gone far from home, the party paused, and Naomi lovingly reminded her daughters-in-law of the facts: she had no more sons for them to marry, they would be better off among their own people, she loved them and wished them well. It was also a decisive moment. Orpah wept, kissed her mother-in-law and Ruth, then went back. Ruth wept and kissed the other two, but she went on with Naomi. Orpah disappeared forever, while Ruth became the ancestress of the Messiah, Jesus Christ.

LOVE TRANSCENDING

Ruth 1: 16-17

16 And Ruth said, Intreat me not to leave thee, or to
return from following after thee: for whither thou
goest, I will go; and where thou lodgest, I will lodge:
thy people shall be my people, and thy God my God:

17 Where thou diest, will I die, and there will I be
buried: the LORD do so to me, and more also, if ought
but death part thee and me.

3

LOVE TRANSCENDING

The words of this passage have been immortalized in music, enshrined in poetry and prose, and read at wedding ceremonies; but they were originally spoken to a mother-in-law.

Orpah was disappearing down the road to Moab, Ruth stood with Naomi watching her go. To both women Naomi had said, go back, I can offer you nothing, You are still of marriageable age, to which she could have added, and not likely to find husbands in Bethlehem. Orpah and Ruth were Moabites, enemies of Israel; and an uncertain reception lay ahead, if they went on with their mother-in-law. In addition, widows were looked upon with suspicion, as possible contributors to their husband's deaths and especially if they were young and childless. So Naomi's love for her daughters-in-law can be seen as she endeavors to convince them to leave her, though she is already lonely and bitter with grief.

Orpah took the advice and with tears streaming down her cheeks, kissed Naomi and started down the road to Moab. Now it was Ruth's turn. She, too, was crying and holding her mother-in-law in an embrace she would not release. "See, your sister-in-law is going home . . . go with her," cried Naomi. In response came the famous and beautiful cry, "Intreat me not to leave thee, or to return from following after thee; for whither thou goest, I will go; and where thou lodgest, I will lodge: thy people shall be my people, and thy God my God. Where thou diest, will I die, and there will I be buried." Love transcending!

Note the character displayed by Ruth, the choice she made, and the completeness of her decision.

The Character Displayed

Who can read these words without admiration for the nobility and humility woven through them?

The nobility is a surprise. Ruth was the product of a degraded race, the children of Moab. The race began with the incestuous episode between drunken Lot and his daughters in a cave outside the smoking ruins of Sodom. Moab was the child of Lot's oldest daughter; and Ammon, the ancestor of another degraded people, was born to the youngest girl. Could any good or noble person come out of such a background? We say no. It is too much to expect. The hereditary and environmental factors are too powerful, and humanly speaking, such conclusions are possibly correct.

"But God . . ." Two little words that make a large difference. They are taken from Ephesians, chapter two. Paul portrays the degradation and hopelessness of us Gentiles: "Dead in trespasses and sins . . . the children of disobedience . . . fulfilling the desires of the flesh . . . the children of wrath." What a pedigree! In the following verses he pictures our position by nature, so much like Ruth's, "without . . . aliens . . . strangers . . . no hope . . . without God." Who could do anything with material like that? The answer is the first two words of verse four, "But God . . . ."

God took a woman, an outsider, a pagan, from an ignoble race and made her the noble ancestress of Messiah. God took us, outsiders, sinners, fallen and depraved and, by grace, made us noble in Christ, "accepted in the Beloved."

The world cynically cries, "You can't change human nature," but God does it all the time. A young woman from an ignoble race, utters noble words which have been and will be repeated as long as man is on this earth.

Along with that nobility, did you see Ruth's humility? "Whither thou goest, I will go," or You lead Naomi, I will follow. Because she took the lowly place, God exalted her. James, the half-brother of Jesus — at first unwilling to accept his relative's Messiahship, but changed after Jesus' resurrection (1 Corinthians 15:7) — learned the lesson of lowliness. He wrote, "God resisteth the proud, but giveth grace unto the humble. Submit yourselves therefore to God" (James 4:6,7). Peter, who was unwilling to submit to anyone before he was faced with his weakness in the crowing of a rooster, wrote, "Yea, all of you be subject one to another, and be clothed with humility; for God resisteth the proud, and giveth grace to the humble" (1 Peter 5:5).

Ruth exemplified this truth hundreds of years before James and Peter, when she said, "Whither thou goest, I will go." A noble, humble woman.

The choice Ruth made was one of those turning points in history, although unknown and unappreciated at the time. Caesar's crossing of the Rubicon and Columbus' decision to keep on sailing westward "one more day" were decisions which dramatically affected history; but no decision ever had a greater impact on humanity than Ruth's decision to go to Bethlehem with Naomi rather than return to Moab with Orpah. God had a plan for Ruth. Our Saviour and our salvation were involved. Messiah was to be born through the offspring of this woman. Now everything hinged on the decision of this moment.

"God would have done it anyway," some will say, "Ruth was predestined to make the correct decision." To this we must partially agree, but her will was involved. She was not a robot or a machine. The mystery of divine sovereignty and human responsibility will never be completely unravelled until we stand before the eternal throne. Orpah made a choice, and so did Ruth; and we are called to do so as well. The choices we make affect our destinies and those who follow after us, for good or evil. "Intreat me not to leave thee." The die was cast. They would go to Bethlehem and into the fabric of human history.

To see how complete that decision was, we need to examine Ruth's statement in detail. She made six affirmations, covering her whole life, and this is a pattern for us to follow.

"Whither thou goest," or my life's direction is in your hands. Centuries later, the God-man born of her lineage would say, "Nevertheless not my will, but Thine be done."

"Where thou lodgest," or the supply of my basic needs is in your hands. Her great-grandson, David, would say, "I have been young, and now am old: yet have I not seen the righteous forsaken, nor his seed begging bread" (Psalm 37:25).

Thy people shall be my people," or nothing shall come between us, not even my family. Jesus met a man who said he wanted to be a follower but first had to bury his father. What he meant was that he would follow Jesus after his father died. Filial devotion came first — to which the Lord replied, "Let the dead bury the dead," or if you will follow me there can be no "ifs" "ands" or "buts." Even family takes a subordinate role.

"Thy God, my God." The hardest statement of all. Ruth was turning her back on all she had been taught since childhood. Of all the ties that are difficult to break, religion is the most difficult. But Jehovah will not share allegiance with the gods of Moab; Christ will not be synthesized with others. The break with the past must be clean and complete — "Thy God, my God."

"Where thou diest, will I die." This is for life! There will be no turning back, no provision for a possible return to the former life if things don't work out in the new land. It is all the way to the grave, the dedication of a lifetime.

"And there will I be buried," or even death will not separate us, Naomi. Centuries later the Holy Spirit through Paul would remind the Roman Christians and us, "For I am persuaded that neither death, nor life, nor angels, nor principalities, nor powers, nor things present, nor things to come, nor height, nor depth, nor any other created thing, shall be able to separate us from the love of God, which is in Christ Jesus our Lord" (Romans 8:38,39). The decisions made on our Moabite road are for eternity. Death and the grave are but entrances to the fulness of what we begin in our earthly life.

And so Orpah disappears into oblivion, but Ruth and Naomi begin their long walk to Bethlehem and history.

BARLEY HARVEST
IN BETHLEHEM

Ruth 1: 19-22

19 So they two went until they came to Beth-lehem. And it came to pass, when they were come to Beth-lehem, that all the city was moved about them, and they said. Is this Na-o-mi?

20 And she said unto them, Call me not Na-o-mi, call me Mar-a: for the Almighty hath dealt very bitterly with me.

21 I went out full, and the LORD hath brought me home again empty: why then call ye me Na-o-mi, seeing the LORD hath testified against me, and the Almighty hath afflicted me?

22 So Na-o-mi returned, and Ruth the Moabitess, her daughter in law, with her, which returned out of the country of Moab: and they came to Beth-lehem in the beginning of barley harvest.

4

BARLEY HARVEST IN BETHLEHEM

Bethlehem at last! Naomi is home again, Ruth is on the threshold of a new life. How long the journey took we are not told. The whole trip is encompassed in one terse sentence, "So they two went until they came to Bethlehem." How many weary days and apprehensive nights, how many bumps and bruises, how much of tears and laughter are wrapped up in that one sentence we will never know, because the Holy Spirit wasn't writing a romantic tale for our pleasure, but He authored a historical report for our admonition. New Testament truth is enfolded in the Old Testament pages, just as Old Testament events lie unfolded in the New. The Book of Ruth is no exception. Notice the calendar when the women arrived in Bethlehem, the climax to which it points us, and the conclusions we may draw.

The Calendar

"They came to Bethlehem in the beginning of barley harvest."

This places the arrival of Ruth and Naomi in the early springtime. The barley was the first of the ripening grains — the "first fruits" so often referred to in the Scriptures.

To appreciate its importance, turn to the Book of Leviticus, chapter twenty-three and study the calendar of the feasts God gave to His people. First came the Passover, on the fourteenth day of the first month. It was a memorial of their redemption from Egyptian slavery. A lamb was slain because salvation was obtained by faith, through shed blood. Shed blood meant a sacrificed life, "Christ our Passover is sacrificed for us" (1 Corinthians 5:7). Then on the following day (15th) was the feast of Unleavened Bread — symbolizing fellowship, with no leaven, which is always a type of sin. In other words, a holy walk of fellowship is to follow our redemption and deliverance by blood.

The third feast was the "First fruits." It took place on the day after the sabbath (our Sunday), "Christ the first fruits, afterward they that are Christ's at His coming" (1 Corinthians 15:23). The long, dark winter is over, the new life of spring is appearing and the first fruits of the coming harvest are offered to God. It was "barley harvest" in Bethlehem when Ruth arrived. The first fruits were being celebrated, and the first thing Ruth did was join the reapers, "Let me now go to the field and glean."(2:2).

How all this illustrates New Testament truth can be seen when we remember that Jesus spoke of *this age* as *the harvest.* In Matthew chapter thirteen, our Lord gave a series of parables that preview this age from its beginning with the sowing of the seed until its end in judgment. In verses thirty-six through thirty-nine, Jesus gives explanations to His disciples, which He did not give the unbelieving crowd: "The field is the world, the good seed are the children of the kingdom" (compare that with verses nineteen through twenty-three, where the seed is called the "word of the kingdom" and the complete picture appears. The seed sown in this age is the Word of God spoken and lived by the "children of the kingdom"), "the harvest is the consummation of the age"; but long before the consummation, the full harvest, was the "first fruits," a promise of things to come. Christ's resurrection was our "first fruits"; and when we by faith identify with Him as our sinless substitute, we are joined with Him in His resurrection (Ephesians 2:5,6).

The Climax

We, like Ruth, have arrived at the time of the first fruits and we, like Ruth, must go into the harvest fields to help the reapers until the full harvest has been reaped at the consummation of this age.

This age, between the first fruits and the full harvest, between the sufferings of Christ and His glorification, was not seen by the Old Testament prophets. As Paul said in Ephesians, chapter three, it "was not made known unto the sons of men, as it is now revealed unto His holy apostles and prophets by the Spirit." That Gentiles should be included in this harvest would have been un- thinkable to the patriarchs of Israel. Indeed, this whole age of grace is nowhere found in Old Testa- ment prophecy. When, on one of His visits to Nazareth, Jesus read in the synagogue from the prophecy of Isaiah, He stopped at the words, "the acceptable year of the Lord." But those were not Isaiah's final words! The prophet wrote, "and the day of vengeance of our God." Why did Jesus stop? Because this is the age of *acceptance.* We are in- volved, or should be, in sowing and watering the seed of the Word of God in the minds and hearts of our fellow men. We were brought in at the barley harvest, the first fruits, so that we may participate in the harvest to come. The day of "vengeance" will come, but not until the Master's harvest is complete. Ruth arrived in Bethlehem at barley harvest and immediately went into the harvest field.

A poll of evangelical churches conducted within the last few years revealed that the greatest percen- tage had contributed few, if any, full-time Chris- tian workers to the needy fields of the world. The poll also showed this sad truth, that most of those who did go into Christian service went to the areas where a substantial number were already at work instead of going to the fields undeveloped and undermanned. No one will argue with the statement that Christians are needed in the professions and the arts in this country. But where is the justice in the fact that ninety-five percent of the Christian workers are serving among the five percent of the world's population who have heard and can hear of Christ, while five percent work among the ninety-five percent of earth's peoples who have not and cannot hear of our Lord?

Modern Ruth, where are you? Out of wicked Moab, into Bethlehem "the house of bread"; out of the depravity and degradation of your past, into the fellowship of the body of Christ! Modern Ruth, is it enough that you're doing? Gazing with interest at the over-burdened reapers in the fields, promising to pray for them and send occasional gifts to them, but never getting your hands dirty with them? The original Ruth's first request, was "Let me now go to the field and glean . . .." Should it not be yours?

Conclusions

There are obligations that follow grace. One of the most important is that we become involved in the business of Him Who has been gracious to us. Naomi brought Ruth to Bethlehem; but Ruth did not assume the attitude, "now what are you going to do for me?" She immediately sought a way to help: grateful love always does. There was a harvest to be brought in. Ruth, by her active participation in the harvest, found that her own long term needs were supplied. Grace will bring me into Bethlehem, but obedience and hard work will bring to me the benefits to be enjoyed. When God brought Israel out of Egypt, He rolled apart the waters of the Red Sea and prepared a dry path crossing place for them: all without one action on the people's part. That is grace. But when the same nation would enter Canaan, the place of rest and fruitfulness, they had to march forward, in obedience to the divine command, toward the river Jordan in flood. There was no advance parting of the waters this time; and, if they had stopped, the Jordan would have continued its flow unperturbed. The blessings of the promised land would have remained untouched, until another, more obedient generation, fulfilled the divine command and trusted God to make a way where there was no way. Only when the priests' feet touched the water; only when they reached the point of "no turning back", did the waters part and the land of God's blessing open to them.

Could it be that the powerlessness of modern, evangelical Christianity can be accounted for by the fact that its people are constantly taking in, but seldom giving out? They analyze, computerize, and theorize about the harvest, but few do any reaping? Like Israel they stand surveying the river, measuring its depth, admiring what is beyond and holding weekly picnics on the bank. Out of Egypt, out of bondage, never to return, but not into the full life God intended for them.

Grateful love, like Ruth's, says "Thank you, Lord, for bringing me into this new life, now what can I do to help?" To which the Master replies, "Go ye into all the world and preach the gospel to every creature." It is barley harvest in Bethlehem, will you join the reapers?

A HAPPY HAP

Ruth 2:3

3 And she went, and came, and gleaned in the field
after the reapers: and her hap was to light on a part of
the field belonging unto Bo-az, who was of the kin-
dred of E-lim-e-lech.

5

A HAPPY HAP

"And her *hap* was to light on a part of the field belonging unto Boaz."

Not all of life's "haps" are happy. The little word used in this verse comes from an Anglo-Saxon word meaning luck, chance, fortune good or bad. It has produced happenings, haphazard, happenstance, happiness, unhappiness, etc. When fortune smiles and luck is good, "hap!" When sickness strikes and the stock market dives, that is also "hap!"

On Ruth's first day in the fields of Bethlehem she was met by a "hap." Her "hap" was to wander into the field of Boaz, and that was a happy "hap" indeed.

Consider the circumstances: she was a childless, penniless, Gentile widow, a member of a cursed race; when she heard the gospel, that the God of Israel had visited His people and given them food. She believed and trusted that message; and, turning her back on her former life, completely committed herself to the new one, even to death. Now Ruth is discovering how God provides for those who put their trust in Him. What a beautiful, illustrative picture of all who through the centuries have heard, responded, and followed the Lord. God had prepared a field for Ruth, Ruth had prepared her heart; and both were united in divine provision. A happy "hap."

The Field Prepared

" . . . the field belonging unto Boaz." Of all the fields around Bethlehem, Ruth chose this one, the field of Boaz, a kinsman through marriage. That the choice was not calculated or deliberate can be seen by the wording of verse three. Ruth had no ulterior motives, only a desire to help in the harvest and be repaid with food for Naomi and herself.

Boaz, whose name means "mighty man," a man of wealth and a kinsman, was the one man in Bethlehem who could do for Ruth what she needed most, redemption. When Elimelech took his family to Moab, he left a mortgage and debts behind. Now Naomi and Ruth (because she married Elimelech's son) must meet those obligations. Under Jewish law the debt could remain in force until the year of jubilee; at which time all debts were canceled, and there was to be a new beginning for all. But the year of jubilee came around only once in fifty years! By that time, Naomi could be dead, the property sold, and Ruth in servitude. So a provision for redemption for those who could not redeem themselves was written into the law. If a near kinsman of sufficient means could be found, who would be willing to pay the redemptive price; he could pay the debt and release the debtor from any servitude — such a man was Boaz. He was wealthy. He was willing to redeem, as we shall see, and he was acceptable as a near kinsman.

What a beautiful type of our Redeemer, Jesus Christ, this Boaz was.

He was from Bethlehem as was Jesus.

He was a near kinsman as was Jesus: "Forasmuch then as the children are partakers of flesh and blood, He also Himself likewise took part of the same . . . for verily He took not on Him the nature of angels: but He took on Him the seed of Abraham. Wherefore in all things it behooved Him to be made like unto His brethren" (Hebrews 2:14-17).

He was willing to redeem as was Jesus: "He was not willing that any should perish" (2 Peter 3:9).

He was able to redeem as was Jesus: "He is able also to save them to the uttermost who come unto God by Him" (Hebrews 7:25).

He was free of obligations of his own as was Jesus, who could challenge the critical Pharisees with the question, "who convinceth me of sin?" and receive no reply.

Of all the fields around Bethlehem "her hap was to light on a part of the field belonging to Boaz," that was no mere coincidence: reminding us of Jesus' statement in John, chapter six and verse thirty-seven, "All that the Father giveth me shall come to me; and him that cometh to me, I will in no wise cast out." That field had been prepared for Ruth from eternity.

The Heart Prepared

The heart of Ruth is seen in verse two of chapter two, "Let me now go to the field . . . go my daughter."

Ruth was a grown woman. She had been married and had her own home. And those were days in Israel when authority had broken down, and permissiveness was the pattern for living; yet here she was asking permission to go to the fields, and from her mother-in-law, no less! What is wrong with Ruth? She was obviously "square," not "with it," and had not heard of "liberation" and the "new morality."

This Moabite showed respect for age and experience. Peter wrote: "ye younger, submit yourselves unto the elder" (1 Peter 5:5). Why? Because they are a source of counsel, direction, experience, and inspiration. It takes many years to learn how to live, and it is a waste not to draw from those wells of accumulated experience. The late George Bernard Shaw is quoted as saying, "What a shame it is to waste youth on young people who don't know how to use it."

Ruth knew that Naomi knew when she should go to the fields. She respected the older woman's experience and position as senior in the home and therefore was submissive and obedient — rare qualities in Israel in that day and equally rare in the church today.

Guidance Prepared

". . . her hap . . ." was no accident, capricious fortune, or blind chance. There were no fences dividing the fields, only boundary markers. No sign proclaimed, "Boaz, Inc. Visitors welcome." Why then did Ruth pick this field? The answer is found in Proverbs, chapter four: "The path of the just is as the shining light, that shineth more and more unto the perfect day." This was the guidance of God. As Isaiah said, "Thine ears shall hear a word behind thee saying, this is the way, walk ye in it, when ye turn to the right hand, and when ye turn to the left" (Isaiah 30:21).

God leads and guides His own. The redeemer, Boaz, had been provided. Ruth's heart had been prepared. Now the Lord will bring the two together in the right field, at the right time, under the right circumstances.

We can learn some valuable lessons concerning divine guidance from the story of Ruth. One, our heart must be right. Pride, obstinance, and rebellion all frustrate our enjoyment of walking the path ordained for us. Someone has wisely said, "Those who have not learned to follow, will never be equipped to lead." Two, the will of God is most often revealed to those who are fulfilling their obligations. Ruth did not hear a voice calling her to the field of Boaz. No golden arrow suddenly appeared on the wall, pointed in the appropriate direction. She was not sitting in a lotus position, mind blank, when the whole picture appeared before her. No! Ruth was out looking for work, willing to take even the menial position of following the reapers, providing food for her mother-in-law and herself, when "her hap" occurred. The Bible, from Genesis to Revelation, pictures God revealing His will to busy people, who are busy fulfilling their obligations. God called Abram while he carried on his life in Ur of Chaldee. He called David from leading sheep. Isaiah was busy with his temple duties, when the divine commission came. Jesus picked busy fishermen and an agent of the Internal Revenue to be His followers. The will of God is not found by sinking within one's self; that is the recipe for despair. The will of God is enjoyed by those whose hearts are right as they live life, caring about others and desire His glory above all.

Then we know a happy "hap."

THE BLESSING

Ruth 2:4,5

4 And, behold, Bo-az came from Beth-lehem, and said unto the reapers, The LORD be with you. And they answered him, The LORD bless thee.

5 Then said Bo-az unto his servant that was set over the reapers. Whose damsel is this?

6

THE BLESSING

What a pleasant surprise these words must have been. Having lived in Moab, a degenerate society, having arrived in Bethlehem in a day of anarchy, immorality, and cruelty; Ruth must have been prepared for cursing, suggestive remarks, or stolid indifference from the other reapers when she came to reap in the field of Boaz. But instead, she heard the master say, "The Lord be with you" and the reapers respond, "The Lord bless you." In the providence of God, Ruth found herself in an oasis of blessing surrounded by a desert of cursing.

So once again, we see God acting to accomplish His purposes in this young woman's life. From her reception to her restriction, we see lessons that apply to us today.

Ruth Received

From the question, "Whose damsel is this?" to the statement, "So Boaz took Ruth and she was his wife" we follow Ruth into the house and family God had prepared for her.

All of this came about because Ruth believed and followed the Word of God. In so doing, she cut her old ties, abandoned her former life, turned her back on old friends, and set her face toward Bethlehem, God's "house of bread."

It is believing and obeying the Word of God which opens the door to *forgiveness.* As Paul said in the synagogue at Antioch, "And by Him all that believe are justified from all things, from which ye could not be justified by the law of Moses" (Acts 13:39). All through that sermon, the Apostle quotes from the Old Testament Scriptures and Christ's fulfillment of them. Believing and obeying God's Word brings forgiveness.

Believing and obeying the Word of God brings us *new life.* The Apostle Peter wrote, "Being born again, . . . by the Word of God, which liveth and abideth forever" (1 Peter 1:23).

Believing and obeying the Word of God had removed Ruth from her pagan life and placed her among the people of God.

This resulted in fellowship and supply. There was no resentment of the "foreigner," no selfish complaint, "when there is so much need here, why do we give to this pagan?" Boaz assured Ruth of safety (vs.9), provided her with food (vs.14), and arranged for grain to be dropped by the "handfuls" where she would pick it up (vs.16).

What a beautiful and accurate picture of our reception by the grace of God. We, too, were strangers, pagans, who believed and obeyed God's word. When we turned from sin to the Saviour, we received forgiveness, new life, and "handfuls of purpose" in the supply of every need.

Ruth Recognized

"Whose damsel is this?"

Who would have expected this? When Ruth left Naomi's house for the barley fields she would have been grateful to be tolerated, to be allowed to pick up the leftovers, and at the day's end, to slip home quietly with the results of her labor. But here stood the master, Boaz, the owner of the field, asking about her — a Moabitish widow, a poverty-stricken stranger, only one of a multitude of poor people trying to find food for their families and themselves.

What a picture of God's grace is this. Ruth fell on her knees before Boaz and asked, "Why have I found grace in thine eyes, that thou shouldest take knowledge of me, seeing I am a stranger?" (vs.10).

The truth is that our Master is interested in and loves the poor, the helpless, the despised stranger. In fact, these are the only ones He saves! Jesus told of two men, one a Pharisee and the other a publican, who stood praying before the altar of God. The Pharisee assured the Lord of his goodness, and the publican beat his breast crying, "God be merciful to me a sinner;" and Jesus said it was the publican who went home justified with God. A rich, young ruler left Jesus' presence "sorrowful," while lepers rejoiced over their cleansing. Remember the call of the Saviour, "Come unto me all ye who *labor* and are *heavy laden* and I will give you rest" (Matthew 11:28).

On another occasion, Jesus said, "They that be whole need not a physician, but they that are sick . . . for I am not come to call the righteous, but sinners to repentance" (Matthew 9:12,13).

Just as Boaz recognized and cared about Ruth, unworthy of his attention as she was, so our Lord recognizes, loves, and cares for us in grace.

This incident is not only a picture of grace on the part of the Master, but also a heart-warming demonstration of graciousness by Boaz' servants. They knew who Ruth was, "It is the Moabitish damsel"; they also knew her background, "out of the country of Moab" (vs. 6); yet they uttered not one complaint or criticism. And when their master ordered them to drop some extra grain for Ruth, they willingly did so. The master's true servants follow his grace with their graciousness. Any other attitude grieves our Lord and His Holy Spirit.

Ruth Restricted

Now that Ruth had been recognized and received by Boaz and his servants, she might have assumed that she was free to go where she wanted to go and do what she wanted to do; but such was not the case. "Then said Boaz unto Ruth . . . go not to glean in another field, neither go from here, but abide here close by my maidens" (vs. 8).

Boaz' servants were separate from the other reapers. Remember, these were dark and dangerous days in Israel, and a hint of this is heard in the assurance, "Have not I charged the young men that they shall not touch thee" (vs. 9)?

If Ruth is to enjoy protection, fellowship, and supply, she must be restricted in her relationships to the world beyond the field of Boaz. So it is with God's servants today. In an age of permissiveness, Christians need to be reminded of the command, "Come out from among them, and be ye separate, saith the Lord, and touch not the unclean thing." (2 Corinthians 6:17). There is danger beyond the boundaries of the Master's field, and too many Christians have discovered this truth the hard way. We live in an unfriendly world, controlled, for the time being, by the enemy of our souls, who is delighted by the opportunities granted him by careless Christians to defeat and discourage them.

The command of Boaz was not motivated by selfishness or a desire to deprive Ruth of happiness that she might find outside his realm. It was a command of love. He cared about her, and her welfare was his concern. So it is with our Lord's command to us, not to stray nor to touch the unclean. He loves us, and He would spare us the hurts that He knows we will receive, if we are disobedient. Some Christians have this concept of God, that He is a celestial spoil-sport, Who, as soon as He sees one of His children having fun, snarls, "Stop him: he's having a good time, he's smiling, I don't want that in my family." As a result, they play a game of, "Let's see what I can get away with; before the Lord catches me, and I have to behave."

If Ruth had insisted on walking off of Boaz' property, she could have done so. Boaz would not have stopped her. And our Master will not stop us. Learning the hard way is one thing our Lord allows us to do, if we insist; but the results are both painful and unnecessary. How much better and happier it is for us to obey, "Go not to another field."

Not only is obedience to the command the path of safety, it is also the only sensible way to live. In this life the only time we are completely free is when we are not voluntarily bound.

The musician, who would be free in his music, binds himself to it. Practice replaces pleasure. Hours that could be enjoyed in other pursuits are given to the perfecting of techniques and the memorizing of scores.

When Michelangelo was commissioned to paint the ceiling of the Sistine Chapel, he erected a scaffolding; and, for four years spent most of his days lying on his back, painting. He constructed a cardboard cap that would hold a candle, so he could paint at night; and when the curious came by to watch, he locked the doors of the chapel so as not to be disturbed. The result was a timeless masterpiece admired by lovers of art from that day on. Michelangelo was free in his art, because he was voluntarily bound to it.

If we would be free Christians, we must be disciplined. Moses stood before Pharaoh and delivered God's ultimatum, "Let my people go" — freedom. But when they had their freedom, God brought them to Sinai, the mount of law. Jesus met fishermen and bid them leave their boats and nets, turn their backs on the former life — freedom. Then He said, "Follow me." Paul described himself as a love-slave of Jesus Christ. Ruth had said to Naomi, "Thy people shall be my people," then Naomi listened as Ruth recounted the events of her day ending with the command of Boaz, to which the older woman responded, "It is good, my daughter . . ." (vs. 22).

The separation spoken of in the Scriptures is not negative, legalistic, or repressive. God's people are called upon to separate *from* so that they may separate *to!* Israel was separated *from* Egypt to be separated *to* Caanan. Ruth was separated *from* Moab so she could be separated *to* Bethlehem. She was separated *from* other fields to be separated *to* the field of Boaz. Paul pictures this truth in his letter to the Thessalonians when he reminds his readers that, "ye turned *to* God *from* idols" (1 Thessalonians 1:9).

Separation which is purely negative is counter-productive. If all I do is remove things from my life, I create a vacuum and "nature abhors a vacuum." Sooner or later something must fill the void. How much better it is to expel the harmful, or the useless, by filling my life with the beneficial and the productive. Read Paul's advice to the Philippians in chapter four of that letter, "Whatsoever things are . . ." then he lists nine beautiful, positive graces and concludes, "think on these things." The old and the ugly are replaced by the new and the lovely.

There was so much in Boaz' field, and it was so safe and pleasant, that Ruth had no difficulty in following his command. When we are in love with our Master and see clearly what we possess in Him, separation from the world and its allurements will not be a legal, grudging duty. But it will be a joyful discipline, which we entered into to make us better reapers and fulfilled followers of Him, "Who for the joy that was set before Him endured the cross, despising the shame, and is set down at the right hand of the throne of God" (Hebrews 12:2).

THE NEARER KINSMAN

Ruth 3:12, 13; 4:1-10

12 And now it is true that I am thy near kinsman: howbeit there is a kinsman nearer than I.

13 Tarry this night, and it shall be in the morning, that if he will perform unto thee the part of a kinsman, well; let him do the kinsman's part: but if he will not do the part of a kinsman to thee, then will I do the part of a kinsman to thee, as the LORD liveth: lie down until the morning.

1 Then went Bo-az up to the gate, and sat him down there: and, behold, the kinsman of whom Bo-az spake came by; unto whom he said, Ho, such a one! turn aside, sit down here. And he turned aside, and sat down.

2 And he took ten men of the elders of the city, and said, Sit ye down here. And they sat down.

3 And he said unto the kinsman, Na-o-mi, that is come again out of the country of Moab, selleth a parcel of land, which was our brother E-lim-e-lech's:

4 And I thought to advertise thee, saying, Buy it before the inhabitants, and before the elders of my people. If thou wilt redeem it, redeem it: but if thou wilt not redeem it, then tell me, that I may know: for there is none to redeem it beside thee; and I am after thee. And he said, I will redeem it.

5 Then said Bo-az, What day thou buyest the field of the hand of Na-o-mi, thou must buy it also of Ruth the Moabitess, the wife of the dead, to raise up the name of the dead upon his inheritance.

6 And the kinsman said, I can not redeem it for myself, lest I mar mine own inheritance: redeem thou my right to thyself; for I cannot redeem it.

7 Now this was the manner in former time in Israel concerning redeeming and concerning changing, for to confirm all things; a man plucked off his shoe, and gave it to his neighbour: and this was a testimony in Israel.

8 Therefore the kinsman said unto Bo-az, Buy it for thee. So he drew off his shoe.

9 And Boaz said unto the elders, and unto all the people, Ye are witnesses this day, that I have bought all that was E-lim-e-lech's, and all that was Chi-li-on's and Mah-lon's, of the hand of Na-o-mi.

10 Moreover Ruth the Moabitess, the wife of Mah-lon, have I purchased to be my wife, to raise up the name of the dead upon his inheritance, that the name of the dead be not cut off from among his brethren, and from the gate of his place: ye are witnesses this day.

7

THE NEARER KINSMAN

This is a moment of suspense in the romance of Ruth. Up to this point all had gone well, God's hand was evident in all that had happened. Ruth, from the first day on the road to Bethlehem, when she made her moving decision, "Intreat me not to leave thee" until she found herself in the field of Boaz, the object of his love, is an excellent illustration of the surrendered, obedient Christian believer — delivered, guided, supplied and cared for.

But all is not well! When Ruth said to Boaz, "spread . . . thy skirt over thine handmaid; for thou art a near kinsman" (vs. 9), Boaz replied, "It is true, I am your near kinsman," and Ruth's heart must have leaped for joy. This man whom she loved, and who loved her, could redeem her from the debts of her late husband's family and thereby save her from servitude. He was wealthy enough, he was willing to so do, and now he had assured her that he also fulfilled the third requirement — he was a "near kinsman." Then the blow fell! "There is a kinsman nearer than I. If he can and will do so, he is the one who must redeem you. You will belong to him. Tomorrow we will see."

What a long night that must have been for Ruth. Imagine, if you can, the questions, fears, and apprehensions that drove sleep from her, "Who is he? What is he like? What will he expect of me, what about Boaz? He loves me, and I love him."

Once again, the romance of Ruth is illustrative of the Christian life. We are delivered from the old life with a sense of joy and relief. New provisions fill the aching voids we could not fill before. We see the hand of God leading and guiding our steps into happy "haps." We revel in the love of our Master and sing, "My Jesus I love Thee, I know Thou art mine." Everything is beautiful, *until* we discover there is a "nearer kinsman."

The Description

Who is this "nearer kinsman?" In the Book of Ruth, he is not named, but we know who he is — Paul in the Scriptures tells us his name:

"And so it is written, The first man, Adam, was made a living soul; the last Adam was made a quickening spirit. However, that was not first which is spiritual, but that which is natural; and afterward that which is spiritual. The first man is of the earth earthy; the second man is the Lord from heaven. As is the earthy, such are they also that are earthy; and as is the heavenly, such are they also that are heavenly. And as we have borne the image of the earthy, we shall also bear the image of the heavenly" (1 Corinthians 15:45-49).

Here is the description of our two kinsmen, "the first Adam," and "the last Adam." The "first man" and "the second man."

The "first man" was Adam, the original, natural, failing ancestor of us all. He was here first, he is the "nearer kinsman" and I am a sinner in his line.

Christ is the "second man" and "last Adam." He took on Himself the form of man (my form). He was "in all points tempted like as we are, yet without sin" (Hebrews 4:15). He is my Boaz, my Master, my lover; and just when I think I'm entering the perfect relationship with Him, that "first Adam" shows up and announces, "I was here first: I have prior claim."

He is a selfish character. "I, me, my, mine" are his most used words. Listen to Ruth's nearer kinsman's response when he was challenged by Boaz, "*I* cannot . . . lest *I* mar *mine* own inheritance . . . *I* cannot redeem" The apostle Paul battled his nearer kinsman and described the conflict in Romans, chapter 7. Thirty-three times in that one chapter he uses the personal pronoun "I"!

The first man Adam, by whom I was born the first time into this world, is my old nature, named in the Scriptures, "the flesh" (Galatians 5:17-21). He has prior claim on me as Ruth's nearer kinsman had a prior claim on her. Now the question comes, "Can he and will he redeem?"

The Decision

Ruth's long, anxious night finally gave way to dawn, and, as the sun rose, the elders of Bethlehem gathered at the gate of the city to hear the cases brought before them and render their decisions.

There was a special electricity present that day, for the word had spread, "Boaz has requested a hearing. It has to do with the Moabitish widow and her nearer kinsman." So the crowd gathered to listen and to look. Somewhere in that crowd was Ruth, looking and listening more intently than anyone else; her future was at stake.

When the two men stood before the elders, Boaz uttered his challenge, "The right of redemption is yours. Can you redeem Ruth, and will you do so?" The nearer kinsman's first response was, "I will redeem." How Ruth's heart must have sunken. "Oh no, it can't be. Dear God, why?"

Then Boaz reminded his rival of the price to be paid. "Can you pay it?" "Are you able?" Here is where the nearer kinsman failed, "I cannot redeem it."

The nearer kinsman of us all, the first Adam, has never been able to redeem. After the Fall, he tried by *conscience,* "let your conscience by your guide" was his motto, but a conscience seared by sin is easily silenced; and mankind became so wicked that God had to wash the world with a flood. After the flood, he tried to build a brave, new world by *human government,* but human government twisted by sin leads to anarchy; so God confused human language and scattered man over the earth. After the tower of Babel, man lived under *the promise* of God to Abraham, but this resulted in Egyptian bondage. When God delivered Israel from Egypt He gave them *the law*. Now man knew exactly what was expected of him, what he could and could not do, surely this would produce the promised redemption. It produced Calvary! Creatures murdering their Creator!

So every time natural man tries to produce his own redemption, he utterly fails! The nearer kinsman cannot redeem. Good deeds, good intentions, religion, and all human efforts are not enough.

Only Jesus Christ fulfills the three requirements for a kinsman-redeemer.

> *1. He must be a near-kinsman*
> "Forasmuch then as the children are partakers of flesh and blood, He (Jesus) also took part of the same" (Hebrews 2:14).
> *2. He must be willing to redeem*
> "The Lord . . . is not willing that any should perish, but that all should come to repentance" (2 Peter 3:9).
> *3. He must be able to redeem*
> ". . . by His own blood entered in once into the holy place, having obtained eternal redemption for us" (Hebrews 9:12). ". . . now once in the end of the age hath He appeared to put away sin by the sacrifice of Himself" (Hebrews 9:26).

Jesus Christ, our Boaz, fulfills and meets all the conditions my "flesh" could never meet, and redeems me by His blood.

The Declaration

Ruth's "nearer kinsman" publicly recognized his inability to redeem by removing his shoe and handing it to Boaz. This meant, "I cannot perform the duty, you must stand in my place and do what I cannot do. Ruth is yours to redeem."

What can be learned from this?

1. My old nature has no claim upon me. I belong to my Redeemer. I am as free of the "old man" as *I wish to be!*

> "Likewise, reckon ye also yourselves to be dead indeed unto sin, but alive unto God through Jesus Christ, our Lord. Let not sin, therefore, reign in your mortal body, that ye should obey it in its lusts. Neither yield ye your members as instruments of unrighteousness unto sin, but yield yourselves unto God, as those that are alive from the dead, and your members as instruments of righteousness unto God" (Romans 6:11-13).

The *provision* of Romans 5:17: "For if by one man's offense death reigned by one, much more they who receive abundance of grace and of the gift of righteousness shall reign in life by one, Jesus Christ," is put into *practice* in Romans 6:11-13. God provides the redemption in Christ, I do the reckoning.

2. The "old man" will try every way to regain his lost place. Paul illustrates this with the story of Ishmael and Isaac (Galatians 4:22-31). Ishmael, born of Abram's fleshly attempt to fulfill the promise of God concerning an heir, was the "first born." When Isaac, the child of promise came along, the "first born" (Ishmael) persecuted him and continued the activity until he was "cast out."

3. I must "cast out" the first born, if the child of promise is to grow and prosper as he should. Boaz had to confront and challenge the "nearer kinsman." Abraham had to deal with Hagar's son and his mistake. Paul said, "neither yield ye your members as instruments of unrighteousness" (Romans 6:13) "make not provision for the flesh to fulfill the lusts thereof"(Romans 13:14). I am free as I "reckon" myself to be in Christ. The desire for a holy, unfettered walk with God is born in me by the Holy Spirit, Who indwells me; but the carrying out of that God-implanted desire is my responsibility! If such were not the case, then the many commands of the New Testament epistles are a waste of time and effort. I am given all the weapons and support that I need for victory, but I must use what has been provided, else it is wasted.

POSTSCRIPT

The romance of Ruth is more than just another love story. It is a picture of our redemption in Christ. As Paul said,

"Now all these things happened unto them for examples, and they are written for our admonition, upon whom the ends of the world are come" (1 Corinthians 10:11).

From the moment of her initial decision to leave her old life, until she entered Boaz' house as his wife, she is the illustration of our salvation. We were pagans, outsiders, under the curse, but God in grace called us, delivered us, redeemed us, and joined us to Himself as His beloved bride.

Let us so live as never to embarrass our Bridegroom.

"For I am jealous over you with godly jealousy; for I have espoused you to one husband that I may present you as a chaste virgin to Christ. But I fear, lest by any means, as the serpent beguiled Eve through his subtilty, so your minds should be corrupted from the simplicity that is in Christ" (2 Corinthians 11:1-3)